Shag Party

SHAG PARTY

Cocktails and Appetizers to Seduce and Entertain

Adam Rocke

illustrations by SHAG

SURREY BOOKS   CHICAGO

SHAG PARTY is published by Surrey Books, 230 E. Ohio St., Suite 120, Chicago, IL 60611.

Illustrations by Shag
Designed and typeset by Joan Sommers Design, Chicago
Printed and bound in China by C&C Offset Printing Co., Ltd.

5 4 3

Library of Congress Cataloging-in-Publication Data

Rocke, Adam
    Shag party : cocktails and appetizers to seduce and entertain / Adam Rocke ; illustrations by Shag
        p. cm.
    ISBN 1-57284-043-9
    1. Cocktail parties. 2. Cocktails. 3. Appetizers. I. Shag. II. Title
    TX731.R5375 2001
    642'.4--dc21   2001049626

Distributed to the trade by Publishers Group West.

Illustrations: *The Spoiled Evening*, 1998 (frontispiece); *The Party Crashers*, 1998 (pp. 4–5); Detail from *The Madonna of Mai Kai*, 2000 (p. 7); *A Proposed Calypso Party*, 2000 (pp. 8–9); Detail from *Mallorca: Dr. Scorpio's Lair*, 2000 (pp. 12–13); *Baron Samedi*, 2000 (pp. 16–17); *The Piano Bar*, 1998 (pp. 20–21); *Snake Eyes*, 2001 (pp. 24–25); *Last Table In Vegas*, 2001 (pp. 28–29); *The Rewards of Evil*, 2000 (pp. 32–33); *The Unchecked Anger of Alf Charles (Late of Shrine Azan)*, 2000 (pp. 38–39); *Wives with Knives*, 1997 (pp. 42–43); *Blue Serenade*, 2000 (pp. 46–47); *Jungle Dowrey*, 2000 (pp. 52–53); *The Marquis' Ladyfriend*, 2000 (pp. 58–59); *The Covetous Neighbor*, 2000 (p. 62).

"A" List

INTRODUCTION

Cocktail parties have long evoked the essence of sophistication—the clinking of glasses and crinkling of plastic slipcovers. Your mother gliding into the moonlit living room, skirt billowing with a hint of sea breeze. Perhaps the sounds and smells of swellegance wafted up the banister where you breathed in the heady scent of romance mingled with cheese balls and longed to someday be a part of those enchanted evenings.

Until, that is, you went to college and began to throw parties designed to annoy the neighbors more than entertain your friends. The night wasn't successful if it ended before 3 a.m. or you woke up to find fewer than five strangers passed out on your floor. Cleaning up after one of those shindigs often meant throwing out a couch cushion or two.

But you're all grown up now, and it's time to throw a party with panache. Whether you're the consummate host or you've just stumbled into your kitchen for the first time, we've got the dandiest of drinks to make your friends swoon. And when you imbibe, you need to eat of course . . . just a little something. Banish that Cheese Whiz and don't even think of clam dip. Our stylish hors

d'oeuvres, ranging from New Year's Eve's *Last Dance Cheese Dip* to Club Night's *Elks in Blankets*, are simple yet seductive.

Throwing a South-of- the-Border party? Dig up some mariachi music (or Señor Sinatra's "Down Mexico Way") and light a couple of nine-inch candles decorated with miracle decals to set the mood. Add our Old Baja Guacamole and your guests will be instantly transported to Cabo San Lucas.

No matter what the theme, a bon vivant simply cannot host the quintessential cocktail party without frilly toothpicks. Cruise by your local party store for swizzle sticks (essential for conveying that certain *je ne sais quoi*), cocktail napkins, and glasses. You may even find some snazzy accouterments, like a 6-foot blow-up hula dancer to shake up a Luau. Just make sure to pack her away before Mom stops by. With edibles and potables galore, *Shag Party* delivers everything you need to host eight memorable theme fêtes. Let the reveling begin!

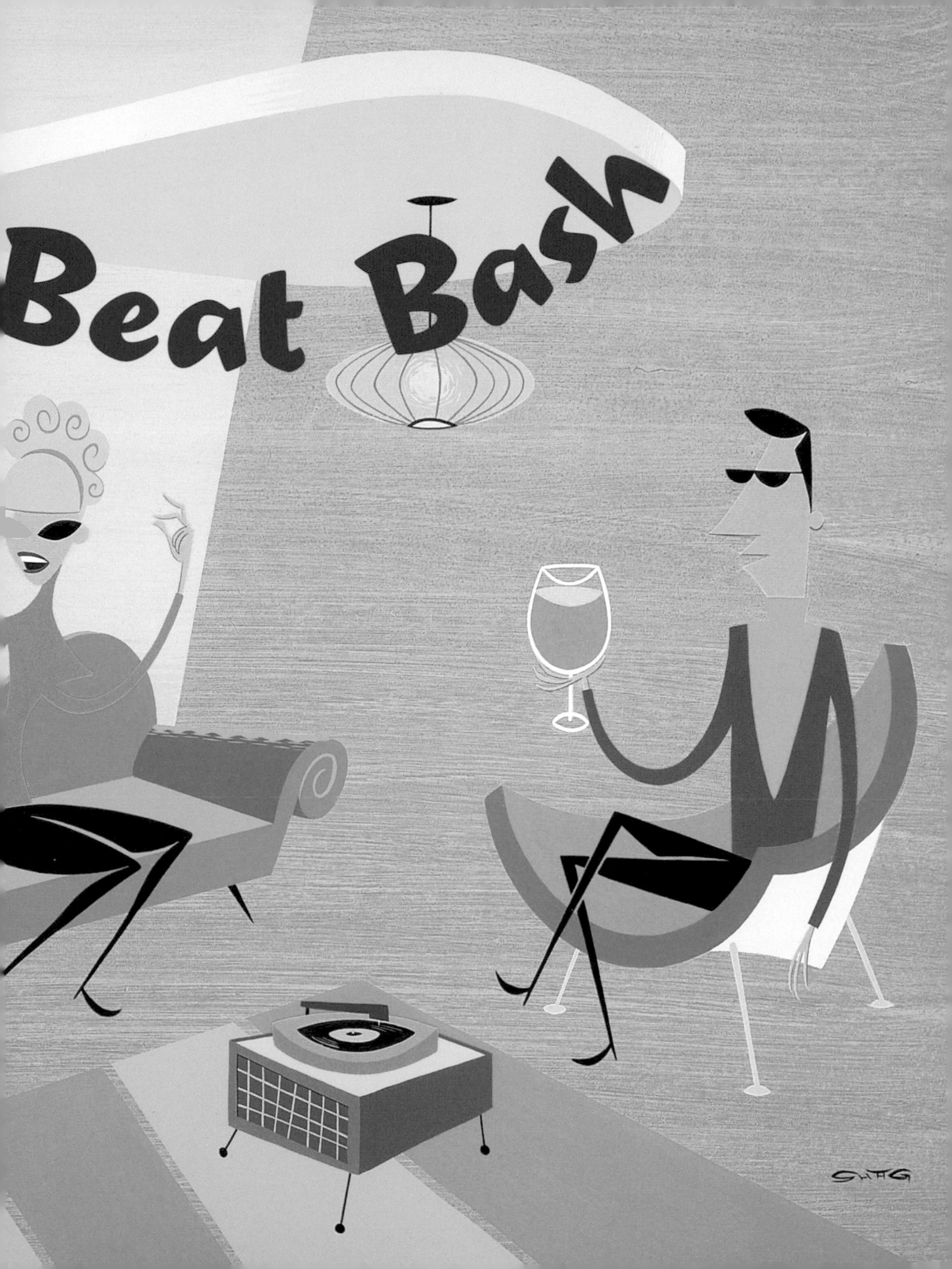
Beat Bash
SHAG

Beat Punch

1 28-ounce bottle light rum
1 pint triple sec
1 quart Hawaiian punch
(or similar multi-fruit juice)
1 pint fresh-squeezed orange juice,
with pulp
Miniature marshmallows

Combine all ingredients,
except marshmallows,
and refrigerate one hour
before serving; pour into a
punch bowl over ice. Float
miniature marshmallows
on top.

Higher Thoughts

1 ½ ounces brandy
1 tablespoon sweet
vermouth
2 teaspoons lemon juice
1 teaspoon grenadine

Old Fashioned glass or snifter;
shake with ice, strain over ice.

Kool Kat Cooler

1 ½ ounces dark rum
¼ ounce triple sec
½ ounce lime juice
1 egg white
Pinch of sugar
Mint leaves

Old Fashioned glass;
shake with ice, strain over
ice. Add mint leaves.

Mondo Martini

1 ounce vodka
½ ounce tequila
½ ounce dry vermouth

Old Fashioned glass; pour over ice,
stir. Orange twist garnish.

Philosophy in a Glass

1 ½ ounces vodka
½ ounce amontillado
medium dry sherry
½ ounce dry vermouth

Cocktail glass; shake with
ice, strain.

Sentient Stix

Serves 8 (6 each)

1 package cream cheese (6 ounces), room temperature

¼ cup chopped scallions

2 teaspoons fresh lemon juice

1–2 teaspoons soy sauce

1–2 teaspoons Dijon mustard

¼ cup chopped pimiento

¼ cup chopped fresh chives

1 clove garlic, minced

6 ribs celery, washed

Process all ingredients, except celery, in a food processor or blender until smooth. Stuff celery with cheese mixture. Cut each rib into 8 pieces.

Hot Dates

Serves 8 (about 4 each)

1 package (8 ounces) pitted dates

1 can (15 ounces) pineapple chunks, drained

1 package bacon, slices cut in half

Place a pineapple chunk in each date; wrap each with half slice of bacon and secure with toothpick. Broil 6 inches from heat source, turning occasionally, until bacon is crisp on all sides. Drain on paper toweling. Serve warm.

Crab Bake de Beauvoir

Serves 8 (about 3 tablespoons each)

8 ounces cottage cheese

1 can (6 ½ ounces) crabmeat, shells removed

2 tablespoons instant chopped onion

½ teaspoon prepared horseradish

½ teaspoon salt

½ teaspoon pepper

2–4 tablespoons milk

Assorted crackers

Combine all ingredients, except crackers, adding enough milk to make dip consistency. Bake at 375 degrees in small baking dish for 15 minutes. Serve hot on crackers.

Kerouac's Hummus

Serves 8 (about 3 tablespoons each)

1 can (15 ounces) chick peas, drained (reserve 2 tablespoons liquid)

⅓ cup tahini (sesame seed paste)

1 large clove garlic, crushed

2–4 tablespoons lemon juice

½ teaspoon salt

1 tablespoon olive oil

1 tablespoon minced parsley

4 pita breads, cut into triangles

Process chick peas with reserved liquid, tahini, garlic, lemon juice, and salt in food processor until smooth; spoon into serving bowl. Make a shallow well in the center; drizzle with olive oil and sprinkle with parsley. Serve with pita triangles.

All Saints Punch

1 quart bourbon
1 quart red wine
1 quart ice tea (unsweetened)
1 pint orange juice
½ pint light rum
½ pint dark rum
¼ pint brandy (use cherry brandy if
cherry syrup is used)
1 cup lemon juice
½ cup lime juice
½ cup cherry syrup (optional)
2 tablespoons vanilla
2 tablespoons sugar

Combine all ingredients, refrigerate over night. Pour over ice into large punch bowl; add more ice tea, if necessary.

Apocalypse Cocktail

1 ½ ounces vodka
1 ounce calvados
½ ounce cognac

Shake with ice, strain into Cocktail glass.

Bloody Martini

1 ½ ounces gin
¼–⅛ ounce dry vermouth
1 tablespoon tomato juice
Dash Tabasco sauce
Pinch salt, to taste

Stir gin and vermouth (or shake for 007!) with ice, strain into Cocktail glass. Add tomato juice, Tabasco sauce, salt. Pimiento-stuffed olive garnish.

Exorcist Cocktail

1 ½ ounces tequila
¾ ounce blue curaçao
¾ ounce lime juice

Shake with ice, strain into Cocktail glass.

Rusty Nail

2 ounces Scotch whiskey
1 ounce Drambuie

Old Fashioned glass; pour over ice, stir.

Ghoulish Ghanoush

Serves 12 (about 3 tablespoons each)

2 large eggplant (about
1 ½ pounds each), peeled
½ cup tahini (sesame
seed paste)
2–4 tablespoons lemon
juice
2 tablespoons olive oil
3 cloves garlic, minced
Salt and pepper, to taste
2 tablespoons sesame
seeds
6 pita breads, cut
into triangles

Slice eggplant into one-inch rounds; microwave at High until very tender, about 5 minutes. Process eggplant, tahini, lemon juice, olive oil, and garlic in food processor until smooth; season to taste with salt and pepper. Refrigerate 2 hours, or overnight. Spoon into bowl, sprinkle with sesame seeds and serve with pita triangles.

Devilish Eggs

Serves 12 (2 halves each)

12 large eggs, hard-cooked, peeled
⅓ cup mayonnaise
1 tablespoon Dijon-style mustard
1 tablespoon red pepper sauce
1 tablespoon dry white wine
Salt and pepper, to taste
Paprika

Cut eggs in half lengthwise, and remove yolks. Mash yolks, mayonnaise, mustard, hot sauce, and wine, making smooth mixture; season to taste with salt and pepper. Spoon filling into egg halves; sprinkle with paprika.

22

E.E.T.'s (Edible Extra-Terrestrials)

Serves 12 (about 3 each)

2 pounds cooked, peeled, deveined shrimp (16–20 count per pound)

1 package (8 ounces) cream cheese, room temperature

1–2 tablespoons wasabi (Japanese horseradish powder)

1–2 tablespoons water

Finely chopped chives or parsley

Split shrimp down the back. Mix cream cheese, wasabi, and water until smooth; spoon about 1½ teaspoons mixture into each shrimp. Sprinkle with chives.

Bat Wings

Serves 12 (about 4 each)

4 pounds chicken wings

1 cup brown sugar, packed

¾ cup sherry

½ teaspoon dry mustard

1 cup soy sauce

2 cloves garlic, minced

Cut tips off chicken wings and discard. Place on baking sheet in a single layer and bake at 350 degrees for 30 minutes. Combine remaining ingredients in saucepan and heat to boiling, stirring until sugar is dissolved. Pour over wings and continue baking 1½ to 2 hours longer, turning wings occasionally, until sauce is absorbed and wings are deeply glazed.

23

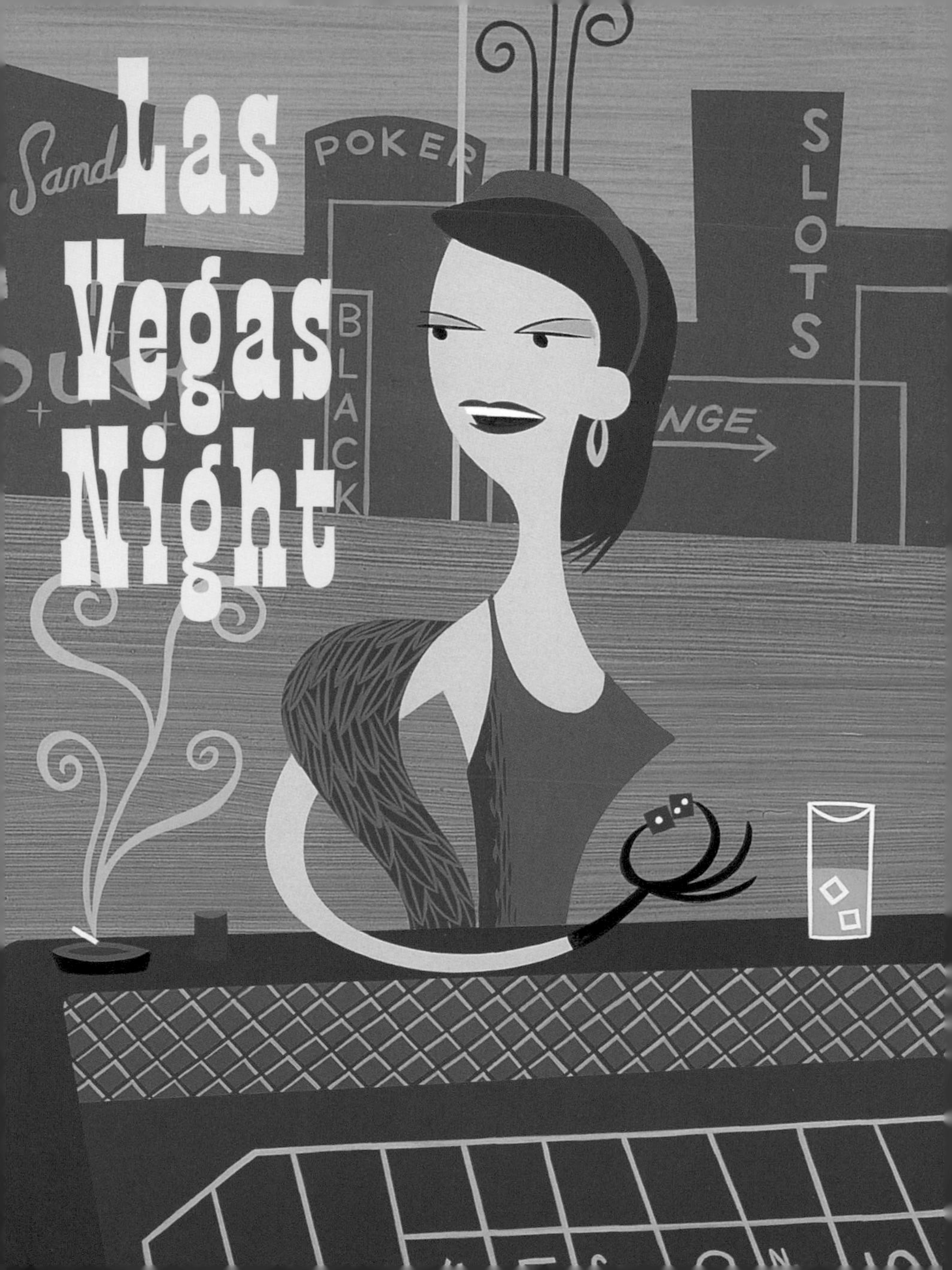

Las Vegas Night
POKER
SLOTS
BLACK
NGE

Hustler

2 ounces bourbon
1 ounce orange curaçao
1 ounce sweet vermouth
2 teaspoons lime juice

Martini or Cocktail glass; shake with ice, strain. Add lemon twist.

Gambler's Cocktail

1 ounce dry gin
½ ounce dry vermouth
½ ounce lemon juice

Cocktail glass; shake with ice, strain. Add lemon twist.

Poker Player's Special

1 ½ ounces rum
1 ½ ounces white crème de menthe

Highball glass; shake with ice, strain over ice.

Russian Roulette

¾ ounce Galliano
½ ounce banana brandy
½ ounce vodka
½ ounce orange juice
1 tablespoon lemon juice

Highball glass; shake with ice, strain over ice.

Blackjack Punch

1 bottle blackberry brandy
1 bottle applejack (apple brandy)
3 cups orange juice
1 cup cranberry juice
1 cup pineapple juice

Combine all ingredients, refrigerate overnight. Pour into punchbowl over ice, serve.

Full House Chutney Spread

Serves 12 (about 2 tablespoons each)

1 package (8 ounces)
cream cheese, softened

⅓ cup mango chutney

2 tablespoons chopped
walnuts, toasted

Whole wheat crackers

Mix cream cheese and chutney
and spoon into bowl; sprinkle with
walnuts. Serve with crackers

Jackpot Crab Mold

Serves 12 (about ⅓ cup each)

1 envelope plain unflavored
gelatin

1 can (10 ½ ounces) cream of
mushroom soup

2 cans (6 ½ ounces each)
crabmeat, shells removed

½ cup finely chopped celery

1 tablespoon finely
chopped onion

1 cup mayonnaise

1 package (8 ounces) cream
cheese, softened

Assorted crackers

Sprinkle gelatin over soup in
saucepan; let stand 5 minutes.
Heat soup just to simmering, stirring constantly. Stir in remaining
ingredients, except crackers;
cook over low heat until cream
cheese is melted, 3 to 4 minutes.
Put into greased 1-quart mold and
refrigerate until set, 3 to 4 hours.
Dip mold briefly into warm water
to loosen; unmold onto serving
plate. Serve with crackers.

High Roller Hot Dogs

Serves 12 (about 2 each)

1 cup tomato puree
3 tablespoons cider vinegar
⅓ cup packed brown sugar
1 ½ teaspoons chili powder
1 clove garlic, peeled and crushed
2 packages (5 ½ ounces each) cocktail franks

Heat all ingredients, except franks, in a skillet and simmer, uncovered, 5 minutes; add franks and simmer until hot through, 3 to 4 minutes, stirring occasionally. Serve warm with toothpicks.

Snake Eyes

Serves 12 (4 each)

2 cups (8 ounces) shredded Cheddar cheese
½ cup butter, softened
1 cup all-purpose flour
1 dash Worcestershire sauce
1 (5 ounce) jar pimiento-stuffed olives

Mix cheese and butter in small bowl until blended; mix in flour and Worcestershire sauce to make a dough. Pinch dough into 48 small balls; flatten with palm of hand, then roll each circle of dough around a stuffed olive. Bake on a lightly greased cookie sheet at 400 degrees for 15 minutes, or until lightly browned.

Cherry Champagne Punch

5 bottles champagne
1 bottle maraschino liqueur
Juice of two lemons
2 cups maraschino cherries
Orange slices

Soak maraschino cherries in maraschino liqueur overnight. 15 minutes prior to serving, pour champagne into ice-filled punch bowl, add all ingredients, stir gently. Float orange slices.

Brandy Alexander

½ ounce white crème de cacao
½ ounce brandy
½ ounce heavy cream
Nutmeg

Cocktail glass (or snifter); shake with ice, strain over ice. Dust with nutmeg.

Chambord Spritzer

1½–2 ounces Chambord
Champagne (chilled)
Club soda

Champagne glass; pour Chambord, add splash of champagne, top with club soda.

Fresh Start

1 ½ ounces Jack Daniels
½ ounce light rum
½ ounce sloe gin
Pineapple juice

Highball glass; pour over ice, fill with pineapple juice, stir. Cherry garnish.

New Year's Cocktail

1 ounce vodka
1 ounce dry vermouth
½ ounce dry gin
2 ounces tomato or V-8 juice
2 drops lemon juice
2 drops Tabasco sauce

Old Fashioned glass; shake with ice, strain over ice.

The 31st

1 ounce vodka
1 ounce cherry brandy
2 teaspoons dry vermouth
1 tablespoon orange juice

Cocktail glass; shake with ice, strain.

Last Dance Cheese Dip

Serves 12 (about ⅓ cup each)

1 pound (4 cups) finely shredded
mild Cheddar cheese

1 pound (4 cups) finely shredded
sharp Cheddar cheese

¼ cup chopped Bermuda onion

1 large clove garlic, peeled

¼ cup catsup

1 tablespoon Worcestershire sauce

⅛ teaspoon hot red pepper sauce

1 can (8-12 ounces) beer

Assorted vegetable relishes
and crackers

Let cheeses stand at room temperature at least 1 hour. Process all ingredients, except beer and assorted relishes, in food processor until smooth. With food processor running, add enough beer to make desired dipping consistency. Refrigerate overnight, or up to 1 week; serve with vegetable relishes and crackers.

Resolution Canapes

Serves 12 (about 2 each)

¼ pound (1 cup) shredded
Cheddar cheese

1 can (8 ounces) minced clams, drained

Pinch cayenne pepper

2 tablespoons chopped parsley

1 tablespoon finely chopped chives
or green onions

24 melba rounds

Combine all ingredients, except melba rounds; spread on melba rounds and broil 4 inches from heat source until cheese is melted, 2 to 3 minutes.

Midnight Meatballs

Serves 12 (about 4 each)

1 pound ground beef chuck
1 medium onion, finely chopped
1 clove garlic, minced
¾ teaspoon salt
1 tablespoon steak sauce
¼ teaspoon pepper
⅛ teaspoon crushed red pepper
¾ cup soft white bread crumbs,
soaked in ¼ cup cold water
1 egg
Dipping sauce: sweet-sour sauce,
plum sauce, mustard sauce

Mix all ingredients, except dipping sauce, and shape into 1-inch balls. Cook meatballs in a greased skillet over medium heat until browned and cooked through, 7 to 10 minutes; drain on paper toweling. Serve with toothpicks and a dipping sauce.

Auld Lang Stuffed Mushrooms

Yield: about 30

1 pound fresh
mushrooms
1 tablespoon chopped
scallions
1 tablespoon butter
½ pint whipping cream
1 tablespoon sherry
½ teaspoon salt
⅛ teaspoon pepper

Wash and dry mushrooms, removing stems. Chop stems and saute with chopped scallions in butter; add cream, sherry, salt and pepper and cook until mixture thickens, about 10 minutes. Fill mushroom caps with the filling and broil until brown and bubbling.

37

CLUB Night

Side Car

1 ounce brandy
½ ounce triple sec
Juice of ¼ lemon

Cocktail glass; shake well with cracked ice, strain.

Manhattan

1 ½ ounces blended whiskey
½ ounce sweet vermouth

Cocktail glass; shake with ice, strain. Cherry garnish. For a **DRY MANHATTAN**, use dry vermouth and garnish with an olive. For a **PERFECT MANHATTAN**, use ¼ ounce each of dry and sweet vermouth and garnish with a lemon twist.

Martini

1 ½ ounces gin
¼–⅛ ounce dry vermouth

Martini or cocktail glass;
stir (or shake for 007!) with
ice, strain. Olive garnish.

Rob Roy

1 ½ ounces Scotch
½–¼ ounce sweet
vermouth

Old Fashioned glass; pour over ice,
stir. Cherry garnish. For DRY ROB
ROY, use dry vermouth and garnish
with an olive. For a PERFECT ROB
ROY, use ¼ ounce each of sweet and
dry vermouth and garnish with a
lemon twist.

Shrimp Cocktail Shriner

Serves 8 (about 4 each)

2 pounds cooked, peeled, deveined shrimp (16 to 20 count per pound)

1 bottle (12 ounces) cocktail sauce

Red pepper sauce

Prepared horseradish

Fill a large bowl with crushed ice. Pour cocktail sauce into small bowl; season to taste with red pepper sauce and horseradish; nest bowl in center of ice. Arrange shrimp on ice. Serve with toothpicks.

Moose Mini Quiche

8 servings (2 each)

1 ¼ cups cottage cheese

¾ cup grated Parmesan cheese

2 tablespoons milk

2 tablespoons flour

½ cup finely chopped fresh spinach

½ teaspoon dried oregano leaves

½ teaspoon dried thyme leaves

Salt and white pepper, to taste

2 eggs

16 frozen, thawed mini-fillo shells

Mix cottage cheese, Parmesan cheese, milk, flour, spinach, oregano, and thyme; season to taste with salt and white pepper. Stir in eggs. Arrange fillo shells on cookie sheet; fill with cheese mixture. Bake at 325 degrees until puffed and beginning to brown on top, about 20 minutes.

Elks in Blankets

Serves 8 (2 each)

1 can (8 ounces) refrigerated crescent roll dough

16 cocktail franks

Dijon mustard

1 large egg beaten with 1 tablespoon milk

1 bottle (12 ounces) chili sauce

Carefully unroll dough, cutting each rectangle into four 3-inch-long strips. Brush each strip lightly with mustard. Roll dough around each frank. Place seam side down on an ungreased baking sheet, about 2 inches apart. Brush dough with egg-milk mixture, and bake at 375 degrees until the dough is puffed and golden, about 15 minutes. Serve with chili sauce.

Rotarian Rumaki

Serves 8 (about 2 each)

2 tablespoons soy sauce

2 tablespoons sake or dry sherry

1 tablespoon grated fresh ginger root

2 teaspoons light brown sugar

8 ounces chicken livers, rinsed

6 thick slices bacon, cut crosswise into thirds

Combine soy sauce, sake, ginger root and brown sugar; pour over chicken livers in bowl. Refrigerate, covered, 1 to 2 hours. Roll each liver in bacon strip, secure with toothpick. Broil 6 inches from heat source, turning occasionally, until bacon is crisp and livers are slightly pink inside. Drain on paper toweling; serve hot.

South of

Sangria

2 bottles dry red wine

2 ounces brandy (flavored optional, to taste)

2 ounces triple sec

1 tablespoon sugar

Club soda

Slices of lemon, lime, orange, and pineapple

Combine all ingredients (except club soda) and refrigerate overnight. Add club soda prior to serving and stir.

Mexican Martini

1 ½ ounces tequila

1 tablespoon dry vermouth

1 teaspoon vanilla extract

Martini or cocktail glass; shake with ice, strain over ice or serve straight up.

Margarita

1 ½ ounces tequila

½ ounce triple sec

1 ounce lemon or lime juice

Cocktail glass; shake with ice, strain into salt-rimmed glass.

Mexico City Fiesta

2 ounces light rum
1 ½ ounces tequila
1 tablespoon orange juice

Old Fashioned glass; shake with ice, strain over ice.

Tequila Sunrise

1 ½ ounces tequila
½ ounce grenadine
2–3 dashes lime juice
2 drops lemon juice
Orange juice

Highball glass; pour tequila, lime and lemon juice over ice. Fill with orange juice. Add grenadine.

White Bull

1 ½ ounces tequila
1 ounce Kahlúa
Cream

Old Fashioned glass; fill with ice, add tequila and Kahlúa, top with cream. Stir gently. Cherry garnish.

49

Old Baja Guacamole

Serves 8 (about ¼ cup each)

4 avocados, peeled, pitted
1 small onion, chopped
1 medium tomato, chopped
½ jalapeño chili, finely chopped
Juice of 1 lime
Salt, to taste
Tortilla chips

Coarsely mash avocado and stir in onion, tomato, and jalapeño chili; season to taste with lime and salt. Serve with tortilla chips.

Jalapeño Poppers

Serves 8 (4 each)

2 packages (8 ounces each) cream cheese, room temperature
1 pound (4 cups) shredded sharp Cheddar cheese
½ cup mayonnaise
18 jalapeño peppers, cut in half lengthwise, seeded
4 eggs, lightly beaten
1 tablespoon milk
3 cups crushed corn flakes

Mix cream cheese, Cheddar cheese, and mayonnaise. Stuff jalapeño halves with the mixture. Mix eggs and milk in small bowl. Dip stuffed jalapeño halves into egg mixture and roll in corn flakes to coat generously. Bake at 350 degrees 30 minutes, or until lightly browned.

Black Bean Salsa Dip

1 can (15 ounces) black beans, rinsed, drained
1/3 cup medium or hot salsa
1 1/2 tablespoons fresh lime juice
1 clove garlic, minced
Garnishes: chopped tomato, cilantro, red bell pepper
Tortilla chips

Process all ingredients, except garnishes and tortilla chips, in food processor or blender until smooth. Spoon into bowl and sprinkle with garnishes; serve with tortilla chips.

Nachos

Serves 8

4 ounces tortilla chips (about 4 cups)
1/4 pound (1 cup) shredded sharp Cheddar cheese
1/4 pound (1 cup) shredded Monterey Jack cheese
1 can (4 ounces) chopped mild green chilies, drained
Garnishes: sour cream, sliced black olives, chopped green onion, cilantro

Spread chips on heatproof pan or platter; sprinkle with cheeses and chilies. Broil 6 inches from heat source until the cheese is melted, 2 to 3 minutes. Top with garnishes and serve warm.

Island Luau

Planter's Punch

2 ounces Myer's dark rum
3 ounces orange juice
Juice of ½ lemon or lime
1 teaspoon sugar
Dash of grenadine

Fill a cocktail shaker with ice, add ingredients, and shake well. Pour into a highball glass and garnish with a maraschino cherry.

Mai Tai

1 ounce light rum
½ ounce triple sec
½ ounce orgeat syrup
1½ ounces sour mix

Highball glass; shake with ice, strain over ice. Cherry and orange slice garnish.

Blue Shark

1½ ounces tequila
1½ ounces vodka
1½ ounces blue Curaçao

Old Fashioned glass; shake with ice, strain over ice.

Piña Colada

1 ½ ounces light rum
1 ounce cream of coconut
2–3 ounces pineapple chunks
(fresh or canned)
2–3 ounces pineapple juice
1 teaspoon light cream
3 ounces crushed ice

Goblet; blend until smooth.
Garnish with cherry and
pineapple wedge.

Scorpion

2 ounces light rum
1 ounce brandy
2 ounces orange juice
½ ounce lemon juice
½ ounce crème de noyaux
3 ounces crushed ice

Highball glass; blend until smooth.
Orange slice garnish.

Paradise

1 ounce gin
1 ounce apricot brandy
1 ½ ounces orange juice

Old Fashioned glass;
shake with ice, strain
over ice.

Crab Rangoon Trader Vic

Serves 6 (4 each)

1 can (6 ½ ounces) crab meat, shells removed

1 package (3 ounces) cream cheese, room temperature

1 teaspoon A-1 sauce

½ teaspoon garlic powder

24 wonton wrappers

Vegetable oil

Mix crab, cream cheese, A-1 sauce, and garlic powder. Place 1 ½ teaspoons mixture in center of wonton wrapper. Moisten the edges of wrapper with water; fold in half diagonally and press edges to seal. Repeat with remaining filling and wonton wrappers. Heat ¼ inch oil in a skillet over medium heat and fry the wontons until lightly browned, 1 to 2 minutes on each side.

Mauna Loa Marbles

Serves 6 (3 each)

1 pound ground pork

½ cup finely chopped water chestnuts

¼ cup finely chopped crystallized ginger

1 egg, lightly beaten

1 teaspoon salt

Cornstarch

Peanut oil

Mix all the ingredients, except cornstarch and peanut oil. Shape the mixture into 18 meatballs; coat lightly with cornstarch. Cook meatballs in greased skillet over medium heat until they are cooked through, 4 to 5 minutes, turning often. Serve hot.

Shrimp Luau

Serves 7 (about 5 each)

2 pounds raw peeled,
deveined shrimp
(16–20 count per pound)
¼ cup lemon juice
1 ½ teaspoons curry powder
¼ teaspoon ground ginger
½ teaspoon salt
1 cup all-purpose flour
⅔ cup milk
2 teaspoons baking powder
Shredded coconut
Oil for deep frying
Sweet-sour or curry sauce

Split the shrimp lengthwise with a sharp knife, but do not cut entirely through. Combine the lemon juice, curry powder, ginger, and salt and pour over shrimp in bowl; refrigerate 1 hour. Mix flour, milk, and baking powder thoroughly. Drain shrimp and add marinade to batter. Coat shrimp with additional flour, dip in the batter, and roll in coconut. Fry in deep oil at 375 degrees until golden brown, 2 to 3 minutes. Serve with sweet-sour or curry sauce.

Pickled Watermelon Rind Papua

Serves 6 (about 3 each)

1 jar (8 ounces) pickled watermelon rind
8 ounces bacon slices, cut in thirds

Wrap pieces of pickled watermelon rind in pieces of bacon and secure with toothpicks. Broil 6 inches from high heat, turning occasionally, until the bacon is crisp. Serve hot.

Seduction for Two

Champagne Cocktail

Chilled champagne
1 sugar cube
Twist of lemon
Dash of bitters

Champagne glass; add ingredients to the glass, fill with champagne.

Sweet Romance

1 ounce vodka
1 ounce light rum
½ ounce apricot brandy
Orange juice

Highball glass; shake with ice, strain over ice. Lemon/lime garnish.

Temptation

2 ounces blended whiskey
¼ ounce triple sec
¼ ounce Pernod
¼ ounce Dubonnet

Cocktail glass; shake with ice, strain.

Love

2 ounces sloe gin
1 egg white
1 teaspoon lemon juice
1 teaspoon raspberry syrup

Old Fashioned glass; shake with ice, strain over ice.

Affair to Remember

½ ounce amaretto
½ ounce triple sec
½ ounce vodka
½ ounce white crème de cacao
1 ounce cream

Old Fashioned glass; shake with ice, strain over ice

Hot Brie from Mars

Serves 2

1 wheel Brie cheese
½ cup slivered almonds
1 tablespoon butter

Saute almonds in butter until golden. Place cheese on serving plate, cover with almonds, and heat in microwave on medium setting until cheese begins to bulge. Serve immediately with water crackers or pumpernickel toast.

Caviar from Venus

Serves 2

¼ cup sour cream
Cocktail rye bread
1 jar (2 ounces) fine quality caviar
1 hard-cooked egg, finely chopped
1 tablespoon finely chopped green onion
2 lemon wedges

Spoon dollops of sour cream on slices of cocktail rye, top each with a spoonful of caviar and garnish with egg, green onion, and a squeeze of lemon juice.

Oysters on the Half Shell

Serves 2 (6 each)

12 cleaned, shucked oysters
Lemon wedges
Parsley sprigs
Cocktail sauce (optional)

Fill large bowl or soup plate with shaved ice, and arrange oysters in shells on ice. Garnish with lemon wedges and parsley. Neophytes dunk in cocktail sauce; aficionados drink the oyster liquor from the shell.

"If Music be the Food of Love..."

Serves 2

1 CD Liszt Hungarian Rhapsody, no. 2
1 CD Rachmaninoff Piano Concerto, no. 2
1 CD Ravel Bolero
1 CD Borodin String Quartet, no. 2

Heat living room to pleasant temperature. Plump sofa pillows. Load disks in CD player, set to eternal replay. Close eyes, pucker up.